t.f.h.

Your First
TURTLE

Louis Dampier

CONTENTS

My thanks to Jerry G. Walls and Ray Hunziker for interesting discussions and ideas, and even some of the words.

Pages 2-3 and 34-35—photos by Robert Zappalorti.

Why a Turtle?

Turtles may be the first reptiles to attract the interest of children. Because turtles are, with very few exceptions, harmless and appealing, parents seldom have objections to children playing with and owning turtles. Their shell or carapace makes them unique among the higher animals, and many species display a marked intelligence, recognizing their owner and knowing when feeding time comes around.

Turtle Problems

But not all is rosy in the turtle world. Because they are so harmless and appealing, in some areas of the world they have been collected too heavily for food or for sale of the shell as souvenirs and various vanity products. Because they are slow and don't fight back, they are ignored as their forests are destroyed and their savannahs and deserts are turned into luxury condos and retirement communities. The water-dwelling species face pollution, dams, motorboats, and death at the hands of "plinkers" with rifles. Any time a turtle comes near a road it faces a good chance of never getting to the other side...none can outrun or dodge a car.

Yet it is possible to keep some types of turtles with few pangs of conscience, because there still are some species that are readily available either as stock bred in captivity or from carefully controlled collecting in areas where the turtles still are abundant and not facing danger. These species adapt well to captivity and with the proper care may live long lives in an attractive terrarium or aquarium. They do not require expensive setups or strange food and will have fewer vet bills than the average dog or cat. The problem is to restrict your interest only to these adaptable species.

This is the purpose of this little book, which is intended as a first reference for the parents of a child of 10 or 12 (because of potential health problems and needed levels of responsibility, turtles may not be suitable pets for younger children). It will help you to make the proper choices and learn which turtles can and cannot be kept by a beginner. If you stay within the recommendations of this book, you should be able to choose a lively, often colorful pet that will require only simple care, will live as good a life as any other pet, and is as environmentally sound as any wild pet can be...and just as much fun.

Land or Water?

Although there are some 240 species or kinds of turtles, they all can be grouped into three basic types: those that live in the sea, those that live mostly on land, and those that are closely tied to the water. The keeping of sea turtles (the only "true" turtles to Britons and Australians) is basically futile and usually illegal, so we can completely ignore the eight or so giant species that comprise the sea turtles. Of the species tied to the land, most are tortoises, members of a group known scientifically as the Testudinidae. (Both Americans and Britons call a tortoise a tortoise, although Britons stretch the name a bit to apply it to box turtles and similar species belonging to other families.) Although advanced hobbyists find the 40 or so species of tortoises fascinating pets that can live long lives and often reproduce in captivity, they present insurmountable problems for beginners: many are endangered; all are subject to serious health problems that demand great care on the part of the keeper; and all are moderately to extremely expensive. After you gain experience with other land turtles you may want to try a tortoise, but remember this list of problems before you do.

Some turtles that spend most of their time on the land do make good pets, however, but they are not really tortoises. These are the American and Asian box turtles and the wood turtles. Several species (a species is a distinctive kind of animal that recognizes others of its own kind and can breed only with other members of its own species under normal

conditions) of box turtles and tropical wood turtles are readily available, often as young animals bred in captivity. Captive-bred box turtles and wood turtles are highly recommended if you can find them.

The majority of the turtles, well over 150 species, are closely tied to the water. Americans call these species water turtles, but they are called terrapins by most Britons and Australians. Some of these, such as the Painted Turtles, the sliders and cooters, Reeves's Turtle, softshells, Stinkpots, and the Snapping Turtle, have long histories as successful pets, although they all have similar problems because of their aquatic lifestyles. All are dirty feeders that produce much waste requiring heavy filtration of the aquarium. Additionally, sliders and cooters are notorious as carriers of salmonella bacteria, a health hazard we'll discuss in more detail later. Juvenile aquatic turtles usually cannot be legally sold in the United States, although they are legally traded in many other countries.

Of some 240 species of turtles, the beginner need only consider some 50 as possible pets. Of these, some are easier to keep than others, some are more attractive, and some are easier to obtain. Your final selection will depend on what is available locally and from mailorder dealers, how much time you have for routine chores, and your personal likes and dislikes.

These turtles **are not** for beginners. Above: The Green Turtle, *Chelonia mydas.* Photo by R. T. Zappalorti. Below: Dwarf and giant tortoises, *Psammobates tentorius* (on back) and *Geochelone pardalis.* Photo by K. H. Switak.

These turtles **are** for beginners. Above: Eastern Box Turtle, *Terrapene carolina.* Photo by R. T. Zappalorti. Below: A Western Painted Turtle, *Chrysemys picta belli.* Photo by R. D. Bartlett.

Housing

In many ways the land-living turtles make more satisfactory pets than do water turtles. This is because a terrarium requires less equipment than an aquarium and is easier to keep clean. Water turtles are notoriously dirty animals, and to keep them presentable you will need a filter of some type and often an indelicate nose to ignore passing smells. Land turtles, on the other hand, can be cleaned up after much like a cat and seldom carry diseases that can be passed on to humans.

Terrariums

For most land turtles you can start out with a simple 50-gallon aquarium. You do not have to purchase an expensive aquarium, as it will not have to hold water. Your local pet shop probably has one or two "leakers" that are in good shape and heavily discounted from normal retail. If you can find an old steel-frame model, rather than the newer all-glass type, buy it—they are much tougher and will withstand a turtle banging its shell against the corners better than an all-glass. They are much heavier, however, and harder to move than an all-glass.

Next you will need a substrate. The substrate is just a fancy way of saying the stuff you put on the bottom to keep the turtle's shell from dragging on the glass or slate bottom of the terrarium. Every keeper has his or her choice of best substrate, everything from ground corncob to peat moss. You must avoid any substrate that is rough or has sharp edges, as these can damage a captive turtle. The most simple substrate probably is newspaper, but it looks bad so is seldom used as more than a temporary measure until a better material can be found. Fine sand works well if you make sure that it does not adhere to the shell of a damp turtle and interfere with regular shedding of the thin horny plates (scutes) that cover the shell. Alfalfa hay is used by some keepers and works well, although it can be hard to clean. Another problem is that it can be contaminated with harmful plants that might be eaten by the turtle. I wouldn't recommend it.

You will need two types of light for the best health of your turtle. One should be an ultraviolet fluorescent light in the proper fixture. Turtles need sunlight, but in captivity sunlight unfiltered by glass (which blocks most of the ultraviolet) may be hard to find. The fluorescent tube will provide a suitable substitute for sunlight, at least sufficient for proper use of vitamins and calcium to ensure proper bone growth. Check with your pet shop to find a light made specifically to supply the needs of reptiles, not plants. The fixture should be long enough to stretch across the terrarium and be fixed securely to the back of the tank. It should be mirrored for best efficiency. Fluorescent bulbs should be replaced every six months to a year to stay efficient.

In one corner of the terrarium you should have a basking area. For most turtles this can be just a clear space, perhaps a shallow box with a couple of inches of sand in it, about double the size of the turtle. Over the basking area suspend an incandescent (tungsten) bulb of at least 20 watts in a photoflood reflector. This will concentrate the heat of the bulb on the basking area and help raise the temperature of the turtle to proper levels so it can function actively. Turtles do not generate as much heat internally as do mammals, and their body temperature reflects the surrounding air temperature. By allowing them to bask whenever they wish, you help duplicate some of their natural behavior patterns. A proper body temperature is essential for a turtle to digest its food completely. Because heaters are hard to maintain in a turtle terrarium (turtle shells can be very destructive of glass heater tubes), most of the heat will be provided by the basking light. Air and floor temperatures in the terrarium should be about 75-80° F during the daytime, dropping five to ten degrees at night for most species; tropical species and those from desert climes may require floor temperatures closer to 90° F. Basking rocks may

reach temperatures over 120° F directly under the bulb, especially with bulbs over 25 watts.

Because your turtle will be confined to an area much smaller than the area it normally calls home, you must provide it with a retreat into which it can escape when captivity causes too much stress. Any opaque box a bit larger than the turtle with an opening of the proper size cut into one side will do, but you will find excellent plastic hide boxes at your dealer. The hide box should be in a cool corner of the terrarium so the turtle can escape the heat of the basking area if it begins to overheat.

Turtles can climb—often surprisingly well—so you should cover the terrarium with wire mesh or something similar that can be securely anchored at the corners to keep the turtle from climbing out. Even a small turtle may be able to climb onto the top of the hide box and stretch enough to push up an unanchored corner. If your turtle can get one front leg over the edge of the terrarium, it probably will be able to pull itself over, crashing to the floor.

To finish your basic terrarium setup you will need a feeding dish, a water dish, and a bathing bowl. Aluminum or pottery pie pans work well for feeding dishes; glass will be broken by the turtle's shell. The water dish should be of pottery, have a large, heavy base, and be small enough so the turtle will not attempt to bathe in it. One of the most annoying problems of keeping turtles is that they will attempt to bathe in

Oddballs: South American side-necked turtles. Above: The terrestrial *Platemys platycephala*. Photo by R. S. Simmons. Below: Hatchling of the aquatic *Hydromedusa tectifera*. Photo by R. D. Bartlett. Both species are fine for moderately advanced hobbyists.

Above: The stunning tropical wood turtle *Rhinoclemmys punctularia*. Photo by J. Visser. Below: An exceptionally attractive Florida Snapping Turtle, *Chelydra serpentina osceola*. Photo by M. Cardwell.

---

their water bowls, spilling water everywhere and causing a general mess.

The bathing bowl should not be in the terrarium but should be kept in some type of waterproof area, such as a tiled room. Most land turtles will insist on bathing for at least two or three hours a day, and some types like to stay in the water half the day or longer. Because turtles like to defecate in their water bath, keep the water clean at all times and keep its surroundings as clean as possible.

Aquariums

The traditional first turtle for children in the United States once was a hatchling Red-eared Slider, *Pseudemys scripta elegans* (don't worry, I'll explain scientific names a bit later). Because of health problems, specifically the fact that small aquatic turtles can transmit a form of food poisoning, salmonellosis, to children, sale of small sliders has been discontinued in the United States although still allowed in many other countries.

The fact remains that water turtles are dirty animals that will turn their aquarium into a cesspool if given the chance. As their keeper, you are responsible for keeping them clean and healthy. This means you need a roomy aquarium with a large filter, frequent water changes, and a basking area.

All the common water turtles are several inches long when adult, so start with at least a 20-gallon aquarium. A "leaker" will not do—you must purchase a good aquarium that holds water. A few gallons of water on the floor make an incredible mess. The tank must be covered with a tight-fitting mesh top to prevent escapes.

Check with your pet dealer about the proper filter to use. You will need a power filter that cleans the water, not a biological filter. You want to remove feces and food wastes as soon as they are deposited. An adequate filter is essential to proper care of a water turtle, and it probably will be your major expense. Since you probably will have only 4 to 10 inches of water in the aquarium, the power filter must be a type that can work in shallow tanks. Recently a self-contained submersible power filter has become available at a reasonable price and works very well in shallow tanks; ordinary power filters require the tank to be filled to near the top. Be sure to supplement the filter with major water changes (about half the volume) once a week and smaller changes daily.

Because turtles constantly dig into the bottom in a futile effort to find natural foods, it is not necessary to provide a substrate as they would just stir it up to dirty the water even more.

Like land turtles, water turtles need two lights over their home. One is an ultraviolet fluorescent fixture specifically designed for reptiles. The other is a basking light over a dry basking area. The same basic setup as described for land turtles can be used, but remember that you need a

DRY basking area, which can be a problem to construct in an aquarium. With small turtles a floating piece of cork or a plastic or wooden shelf anchored to the wall of the aquarium at the water level will work, but larger turtles will destroy such fragile basking areas. Many keepers build a platform of smooth, flat rocks laid one over the other until the water level is reached, the rocks securely anchored with silicone cement. Others build a wooden ramp on one side of the aquarium that allows the turtle to walk up under the light to bask.

Adult water turtles from the Northern Hemisphere usually can be kept at room temperature during the summer, but in the winter they may need supplementary heat. Heaters in the tank are dangerous as they can be crushed. The basking light may provide enough heat to keep the water at 75° F or so, especially if an under-tank heating pad is used to help maintain a fairly constant temperature. As usual, allow the temperature to drop five to ten degrees at night. Young turtles need higher water temperatures than adults.

To measure the temperature you will need a good thermometer. The liquid crystal type that adheres outside the tank is best. Attach it just above the bottom of the tank for best results. If you wish, a second thermometer placed even with the top of the water will allow you to determine the average water temperature accurately.

Except for the softshells, Stinkpots, and Snapping Turtles, all common water turtles have to bask several hours a day both to maintain their temperature and to utilize the vitamins and minerals necessary for their health. Basking also dries the shell, keeping algae under control and making it easier to shed the scutes of the shell without problems.

To help keep everything as clean as possible, do not feed your turtle in its aquarium. Feed it in a separate smaller aquarium or plastic basin of proper size and then let the turtle stay there until it defecates at least once (usually an hour or less after feeding). Many water turtles will only eat when able to submerge completely (otherwise they cannot swallow). Water turtles use their food poorly and seem to be constantly producing feces, which will have to be removed from the tank daily or smelly and dangerous conditions will result within a day or two at the most. You must keep the aquarium clean!

No common water turtle is completely aquatic. They must breathe at the surface, bask in a dry area exposed to sun, and leave the water to lay their eggs. In fact, other than when eating and defecating, most water turtles will do quite well with only limited access to water deep enough in which to swim. They cannot be kept in dry surroundings very long, but they don't really need gallons of water in which to be comfortable.

Above: A young River Cooter, *Pseudemys concinna*. Photo by R. D. Bartlett. Facing Page, Top: Plastron on a young Mexican Wood Turtle, *Rhinoclemmys pulcherrima*. Photo by G. Dingerkus. Facing Page, Bottom: The rare and expensive *Cuora aureocapitata*. Photo by R. D. Bartlett.

Nutrition

Most turtles that are easily kept in captivity will accept a broad array of foods. Few are specialists, which makes the diet easy to arrange.

Basic Foods

For the best nutrition, provide a mixture of greens and animal protein. By this I do not mean lettuce and mealworms, both commonly offered foods that are best avoided except as treats. Greens can consist of almost anything you would want to include in your diet, such as string beans, leaf and chopped spinach, romaine lettuce, chicory, and peas. Avoid the cabbage family of greens, however, as they tend to cause diarrhea in many turtles, and you will have enough of a problem with cleanliness without added complications. Many water turtles like water plants, so try to give them some filamentous algae or pond weeds from an unpolluted pond and see how they like them. A batch of elodea or a similar soft water plant from the pet shop is a food that is readily available at all times of the year. You may find that some species prefer this to all other vegetables and greens. Additionally, water plants often contain small snails and insect larvae like those taken by many water turtles in their natural surroundings.

Fruits of many types are taken by land turtles, including especially the brightly colored fruits such as strawberries, cherries, diced apple, and bits of pear. Bananas are favored by many species, but they turn into a mess if the turtle stomps up and down on them a few times; few turtles eat banana peels, by the way. Box turtles often will eat melon and mushrooms. There is no reason most water turtles would not accept these foods as well, if you can figure out a clean way of offering them.

Although greens are best offered fresh, some turtles will learn to accept canned or frozen and thoroughly thawed veggies, especially string beans, peas, and occasionally even canned peaches. Be sure to thoroughly wash and drain any preserved foods—turtles don't need heavy syrup in their diet.

Animal protein is necessary for most turtles and essential for many species. Stay away from frozen fish if at all possible, especially marine species, as frozen raw fish may lead to vitamin imbalances and even death if fed too often. Whole living fish, such as small goldfish and guppies, will be taken by most water turtles and even many land turtles. They are an excellent source of calcium. Chopped shrimp and clams, if fully drained and washed to remove preservatives and salt, are fine, though messy. Moist catfood pellets are irresistible to some turtles and a good source of protein and an excellent supplement to any diet. For that matter, occasional treats of canned catfood will do wonders for the appetite and temperament of many land turtles. Feeding such messy canned foods to water turtles will be difficult, but sliders and softshells need more protein than do most land turtles.

Many water turtles enjoy snails of all types, deriving additional calcium from the shells. Also enjoyed are crickets, which are an excellent food, cheap, and easily cultured. For that matter, flies, cockroaches, and various other insects are taken by many turtles, but they present the problem of possible pesticide contamination and perhaps are best avoided.

Vitamins

All turtles should be given vitamin supplements (A, B group, C, D) made specifically for reptiles. The supplement should be added to the food on a regular basis following instructions on the container. Always buy vitamins made for reptiles; if you cannot find reptile vitamins, use bird vitamins while continuing to hunt for reptile vitamins. Because of certain details of their metabolism, turtles may not be able to completely utilize vitamin mixtures designed for hamsters, gerbils, humans, and other mammals.

If you feed a powdered supplement, it can be added to the greens and meat you are feeding your land turtle (the "salad," as it often is called) by simply sprinkling it over the food, which should be slightly moistened. Crickets can be moistened a bit and then sprinkled with vitamins, plus they can be fed a diet spiked with vitamins. It is more difficult to give vitamins to water turtles, although you can try injecting oil-based vitamins into food fishes or even catfood pellets. If you can get your water turtle to eat in a minimum of water, you can try sprinkling vitamin powder onto the food, but it may not work. Vitamins designed to be just dropped into the water probably are worthless.

Calcium

Turtles are largely shell, and thus bone. Bone is basically a calcium and phosphorus compound. You must provide a proper amount of calcium for all turtles, especially rapidly growing young specimens. Water turtles are more subject to calcium deficiencies than land turtles, probably because their captive habitat and diet are always so different from natural conditions.

You cannot just provide calcium and expect your turtle to be healthy. Calcium has to be present in the proper ratio to phosphorus to build strong bones in the presence of vitamin D. Unfortunately, the exact ratio is uncertain for virtually all turtles and probably varies with different captive conditions, individuals, and stress. One of the most often recommended calcium

Above: A juvenile Malayan Box Turtle, *Cuora amboinensis*. Photo by K. T. Nemuras. Facing Page, Top: The bizarre and delicate Black-breasted Leaf Turtle, *Geoemyda spengleri*. Photo by R. D. Bartlett. Facing Page, Bottom: A juvenile map turtle, *Graptemys kohni*, of the southern United States. Photo by K. T. Nemuras.

Insect larvae, such as this caddisfly larva, make excellent treats for aquatic turtles.

supplements is cuttlebone, the type often sold for use in parakeet cages. Some turtles will actually chew off pieces of whole cuttlebone, while others will only accept it in ground form sprinkled over the food. Cuttlefish are a type of squid, and their shell is heavy in salt, which may discourage some species from eating it unless soaked and washed.

Perhaps one of the best calcium supplements is crushed egg shell. Because birds are just reptiles with feathers, their calcium–phosphorus ratio is fairly close to that of turtles. Egg shell is easy to obtain, stores well after boiling, and is eaten greedily by both water and land turtles.

Several commercial calcium supplements for reptiles are available at your dealer and should work. Gypsum turtle blocks probably are worthless as they do not provide the proper calcium–phosphorus ratio.

Feeding Schedules

Land turtles become used to regular feeding times and places,

much as do cats and dogs. Many will rapidly learn to recognize their keeper. Aquatic turtles seldom seem so intelligent, perhaps because of their more restricted habitat.

As a general rule, offer food every other day. Feed each turtle separately to prevent fights and territorial disputes. Many keepers offer veggies and animal protein on alternating days, while others try to offer some of each with every feeding. Turtles with good appetites probably will not suffer from missing a meal every week. If they obviously are putting on too much weight, cut back on the amounts fed and the frequency of feeding.

Don't be afraid to experiment with the diet. Many turtles are attracted to bright colors such as yellow and red, so they may greedily take rose petals, dandelions, and other flowers. Earthworms are fine treats for many land turtles and often will be taken by water turtles as well (especially Stinkpots and Snapping Turtles). Just stay away from frozen fish, marine fishes, salt, sweets, stale food, cabbages, and foods that might be contaminated with pesticides. Prepared turtle foods may be good, but be sure to read the label for nutritional content. If you nibble a bit and don't find it too repulsive, it probably is alright. Never feed prepared foods that smell stale, have begun to fragment into powder, look like they might have fungus spots, or break up too rapidly in water.

Health

If kept in the proper surroundings and given a varied, balanced diet with sufficient vitamin and calcium supplements, the common turtles will remain healthy for years in captivity. In fact, most pet turtles should live at least ten years, and some species, such as the box turtles and tortoises, may easily exceed 50 years. As much as I hate to admit it, if your turtle becomes ill there probably is little you can do about it. Veterinarians who are competent to treat even basic turtle diseases are virtually nonexistent, and the scientific knowledge about turtle diseases is marginal to begin with.

Selection

The first step in having a healthy turtle is to buy only the healthiest specimen you can find. Look at the eyes first. In the common turtles the eyes are bright and glossy, never sunken into the skin and dull. The eyes are indeed the doorway to the soul of the turtle, and they are often the first sign that an illness is developing. Dull eyes—poor turtle. When you pick up the turtle, it should struggle, at least extending the legs in an attempt to stay in touch with the ground. A few species (such as the box turtles) withdraw into the shell when lifted, but when held for a few minutes many will then begin to struggle. Turtles that just let their legs hang down limply when picked up are not long for this world.

If there is any type of pus or mucus around the eyes or nostrils, or if the turtle is breathing loudly and harshly, it probably is sick and should not be purchased. These are signs of various types of bacterial infections that often can be treated with broad-spectrum antibiotics available from your pet shop or veterinarian, but the infections themselves are a sign of poor general health attributable either to poor care or injury during capture. You might be able to cure the infection, but it will recur unless captive conditions are improved.

Shedding problems

Unlike lizards and snakes that shed the skin more or less in one piece, turtles shed the skin of the legs and head almost scale by scale over long periods. The scutes of the carapace (the upper shell) and plastron (lower shell) are shed individually in no obvious order.

It is not uncommon for a turtle to have one or more loose and partially shed scutes. If scutes fail to drop off completely, they may affect the shape of the new scute underneath, resulting in odd, often domed shapes. Such odd shapes are not uncommon in captive turtles and may be unsightly but are not dangerous. Unlike snakes and

Attractive mutations of the Red-eared Slider, *Pseudemys scripta elegans*. Above: A glowing albino. Below: A pastel with reduced pattern. Photos by R. D. Bartlett.

Above: An albino of the endangered Flattened Musk Turtle, *Sternotherus depressus*. Photo by R. D. Bartlett. Below: The Spotted Turtle, *Clemmys guttata,* a close relative of the Wood Turtle. Photo by R. T. Zappalorti.

lizards, turtles seldom have shedding problems unless they are kept under abysmal conditions.

Parasites

The droppings of turtles often contain large numbers of parasitic worms, especially roundworms. These can be eliminated by a few doses of piperazine or a similar mild worming agent such as used for cats and dogs. Worming compounds can be purchased in pet shops or from veterinarians. Small doses given in the food usually work, but go slowly and be observant for side effects. Worms are natural inhabitants of the turtle gut and are constantly being reintroduced with wild foods and from the feces of other turtles.

Occasionally leeches, worms related to earthworms but with a sucking disc at each end, are found attached on the shell or at the bases of the legs and tail of a water turtle. The worms can be removed with tweezers and the wound dabbed with rubbing alcohol or an antibiotic salve to prevent infection. Leeches are disgusting to look at, can cause anemia if present in large numbers (rare), and can transmit parasites.

Salmonellosis

Few other problems have had such far-reaching effects on the turtle hobby as salmonellosis. This disease is a type of food poisoning caused by bacteria of the genera *Salmonella* and *Arizona*, among others, bacteria that are present naturally in the gut and thus in the feces and tank water of virtually all young water turtles. Salmonellosis is especially prevalent in young sliders and cooters (which includes the Red-eared Slider) raised on large turtle farms in the southern United States, where they may be kept in polluted water. The bacteria are transmitted from the mother turtle to the young through the eggs, which makes the disease very difficult to control.

Salmonellosis seldom causes the turtle any problems, but it is quite infectious in humans, especially children who have a tendency to put a small pet turtle in their mouth or put their hand in turtle tank water and then not wash immediately in hot soapy water. In small children the resulting food poisoning can be serious and require hospitalization; a few deaths have resulted. There does not appear to be any way to produce perfectly bacteria-free baby turtles.

Because of the severity of the infection and the inability to prevent it, in 1975 the United States Food and Drug Administration had laws passed to eliminate the shipment of baby Red-ears over state lines and to prevent their sale in stores. The individual states then passed similar legislation, resulting in the virtual inability to legally sell any turtle under 4 inches in shell length anywhere in the United States. Canada has similar laws, but Europe and Japan are still major markets for baby Red-eared Sliders.

The Turtles

Now is the time for you to decide if you want an aquatic turtle or a land turtle, because you will have to set up the new turtle's home correctly as described earlier. You know you will be able to get the proper variety of foods, and you've talked to your pet shop dealer or veterinarian about back-up if your turtle should become ill. If you are the parent of a young child, you have explained to the child that turtles are not toys and not to be played with. You have explained that if they should put the turtle or its water near the mouth or a cut, they may become sick. As a parent, adult, or older child, you are aware of these problems as well. Now, what turtles can you get?

We've already talked about selecting a healthy turtle, so you are looking for a pet with bright eyes and a good, active attitude. Water turtles seldom are handled except to put them into the feeding aquarium and to clean the tank, but this will happen almost every day, so you don't want a turtle that is excessively aggressive. Land turtles seldom are aggressive, and many become real "pussycats" in captivity.

Oh yes—you should get only one turtle, not two or three even if they are cheap. Contrary to what you may have read elsewhere, turtles are not really social animals, although they often will tolerate some company. Turtles are territorial and like to have a home area of their own without competition for food and space. Single turtles produce less waste than do multiple turtles, especially important with the aquatic species restricted to small tanks (and even 20 gallons is small for any turtle).

Your final choice of a turtle will depend to some extent on what is available at local pet shops. Few shops carry a wide variety of turtles, but most shops will gladly order a turtle for you if you know what you want. Turtles seldom are cheap animals, and some species are very expensive, so never be afraid to ask prices. As a beginner, you should stick to one of the cheaper species— cheaper in this case usually means more common and easier to obtain. Mailorder dealers advertise in pet magazines such as *Tropical Fish Hobbyist* and in the newsletters of local herpetology clubs, and they often have more species available than the local pet shop. However, it is always best to actually see and handle a turtle before you buy it.

The addresses of local herpetology (herpetology is the study of reptiles and amphibians) clubs may be obtained through your pet shop, the local high school or college biology department, or the local zoo. Belonging to a local herp club will let you meet others with similar interests.

Above: *Cuora trifasciata,* an attractive Asian box turtle. Photo by K. T. Nemuras.
Facing Page, Top: Reeves's Turtle, *Chinemys reevesi.* Photo by J. Visser.
Facing Page. Bottom: Young Yellowbelly Slider, *Pseudemys scripta scripta.*
Photo by R. D. Bartlett.

Scientific Names

We now have to briefly discuss those Latinized words that make up the official or scientific name of every type of turtle. Every species and often every distinctive type of turtle found within a particular geographic area has its own unique scientific name that allows it to be recognized in any language. Common names such as Red-eared Slider vary from country to country (this is the Red-eared Terrapin in Britain) and often from book to book, making it hard to understand just what turtle is being talked about.

Every scientific name is made up of at least two parts and is written in italic type or at least underlined. The first part of the name, the genus (plural, genera), is capitalized. A genus is a broader group of species that has rather major differences from other genera. Examples are *Pseudemys* for the sliders and cooters, *Geochelone* for many tortoises, and *Chrysemys* for the Painted Turtle. A genus may contain only one species (as does *Chrysemys*) or many (as does *Pseudemys*). The second part of the name is the species (singular and plural—specie refers to money, never animals). Each species should interbreed only with its own type under natural conditions and fits into the ecology of an area in a way different from any other species. Sometimes a scientific name has a third part, the subspecies. A subspecies is like a species but is restricted to only one part of the geographical range of the entire species and interbreeds with other subspecies where they meet. The Red-eared Slider, *Pseudemys scripta elegans*, is a subspecies (*elegans*) of a species (*scripta*) known simply as the Slider. Another subspecies of the Slider is the Yellowbelly Slider, *Pseudemys scripta scripta*, recognized by its more easterly range and a large yellow blotch behind the eye, without red.

Water Turtles

Although they are harder to keep clean, water turtles often are easier to care for than land turtles. Just be sure that they get a varied diet, are kept warm enough, have a good basking area, and get the calcium and vitamins they need for strong shells. In the United States you cannot legally purchase water turtles under about 4 inches shell length because of the salmonellosis problem.

Reeves's Turtle, *Chinemys reevesi,* is an abundant import from China and ranges over much of that country, Korea, and Japan. The carapace (upper shell) has three strong keels, and the overall color is dull olive brown with traces of yellow striping and spotting on the head and neck. Adults vary from 4 to 15 inches in length. Although Reeves's Turtle is not an especially pretty species, it eats almost anything, both plant and animal, does not need high water temperatures (75° F), likes to bask, is gentle, and because it matures at a small size has relatively low calcium demands. Although seldom bred in captivity, it still is common over its natural home area and doesn't seem to suffer from sustained collecting pressure, so it is what could be called an environmentally neutral species. It is still among the cheapest of turtles to purchase. Highly recommended.

The Painted Turtle, *Chrysemys picta*, ranges over much of North America. It is somewhat flat-shelled, has a thick, heavy shell, and often has bright red and yellow stripes on the head and neck plus red areas and even stripes on the shell. The undershell usually is bright yellow. Paints are among the prettiest of common turtles, are extremely adaptable, and mature at a small size (4 inches), topping out at about 7 inches. A Paint needs a lot of plants in its diet if it is to do well, but it also takes animal foods such as snails and small crayfish or the occasional fish. Seldom bred in captivity, it is abundant enough in many areas to support limited collecting without harm, and there is little doubt that it could be easily bred if necessary. Highly recommended.

Sliders and cooters, members of the genus *Pseudemys* (the genus *Trachemys* sometimes is used for the Slider and its relatives), once were the most commonly seen pet turtles on the United States market, and they still are abundant in the pet shops of many other countries. Baby sliders, especially the Red-eared, once were available at under 2 inches in length, when they have the brightest green shell colors, but such little turtles require warm water temperatures, tremendous amounts of calcium, and the finest of foods to survive very long. If they are available to you, they are not recommended as pets for beginners. Larger sliders and cooters tend to have brownish shells and subdued yellow lines on the head; many types are over a foot in length and very difficult to keep in a convenient size of tank. These also are among the dirtiest of turtles, making clean tanks almost impossible to maintain. Recently Red-eared Sliders have been bred in a few color mutations, including an albino in which the red ear stripe is extremely bright, and a "pastel" in which the dark background colors of the shell and head are replaced with pale orange to yellow, resulting in a striking pattern. Adults of these color varieties may be the most attractive water turtles if they are not allowed to overgrow with algae and are kept clean. Sliders and cooters can be recommended only with reservation because of their adult size and the salmonellosis problem affecting young specimens.

Stinkpots, *Sternotherus odoratus*, seldom exceed 4 inches in length, so they seldom are commercially available on the U.S. market, although they are easily collected in most of the eastern United States. Yes, they do tend to exude a foul-smelling anal gland secretion when first collected, but they tame quickly

The Loggerhead Musk Turtle, *Sternotherus minor,* a close relative of the Stinkpot. Photo by K. T. Nemuras.

Hatchling *Mauremys japonica,* a pond turtle from Japan. Photo by R. D. Bartlett.

and become excellent pets. They are extremely aquatic and can be observed walking along the bottom looking for food—they like fish, frogs, snails, earthworms, and other meaty foods, with a bit of vegetation occasionally. Not sensitive to temperatures, they are active even under ice. They seldom bask, but they should be given basking areas for those days when the mood strikes them. Stinkpots are excellent climbers and must be kept in a securely covered tank. Recommended, but not commercially available on a regular basis.

Softshells, family Trionychidae, are generally flattened turtles with long snouts and aggressive temperaments. Large specimens can be ferocious and draw blood. They seldom bask but should be given a basking area anyway. Most species eat animal foods in preference to vegetables. Because the shell lacks bony plates, it is easily scratched by rough stones or even branches, so fungal infections are not uncommon. Keepable, but not recommended for beginners, although advanced hobbyists find them fascinating pets.

The Snapping Turtle, *Chelydra serpentina*, commonly reaches a foot in length and has a massive head with gigantic beaks. The coloration is a plain brown, the attitude is bad, and large specimens can be dangerous. Still, many turtle keepers find this species fascinating, and it certainly is a hardy and long-lived species. Babies are almost black and strongly ridged, with a very long tail. Not recommended for beginners, but to be considered after you have kept a few other species and if you have the room and patience for a big, mean turtle.

Land Turtles

First, do not even consider a tortoise of any type if you are a beginning turtle keeper. Tortoises (*Testudo, Geochelone*, and a few other genera) have very specific temperature and humidity requirements that are difficult to match in captivity without a good bit of knowledge, and many are threatened by development and overcollecting. Most specimens that enter the marketplace die within a year, which is a shame for an animal that may live 40 or 50 years in nature. Tortoises are for specialists. They also are very expensive when you can find them.

Asian box turtles, *Cuora*, are semi-aquatic turtles from tropical Asia that adapt well to terrariums if allowed to bathe and bask often. Most of the species have a well-developed hinge near the center of the plastron that allows the turtle to retract the head and legs and then close up the shell for protection. Once they become used to their keeper, they seldom close up. Some species are very attractive, with bright head patterns and attractive shells. The Malayan Box Turtle, *Cuora amboinensis*, often is available at a reasonable price. It is something of a vegetarian but in captivity learns to eat animal protein as well. More aquatic than the American box turtles, it should be allowed to bathe whenever it wants. Provide a basking area. Since it seldom exceeds 8 inches in length, it is a nice size for a pet. Recommended.

American box turtles, *Terrapene*, make excellent pets if you can get one, but most specimens are collected and not bred in captivity. Because of land development and losses to automobile traffic, box turtles have become less common in many parts of their range and are considered threatened in some American states. Two common species (the Eastern, *T. carolina*, and the Western or Ornate, *T. ornata*) are found in fields and prairies, with the Eastern Box Turtle also common near forests. Both are high-domed, have hinged lower shells that allow them to close up tightly, and like colorful berries and flowers plus fruits such as melon and apple. Both need basking and bathing areas and can be very friendly and hardy pets. Recommended only if you can get a specimen that was bred in captivity.

Wood turtles are of two types. The true Wood Turtle, *Clemmys insculpta*, is a native of northeastern North America, being found near rivers and in damp fields and marshes. At 8 inches, it is a heavy, active, very intelligent turtle though not especially colorful (brown, with tinges of red). Considered by many to be one of the best pet turtles, it unfortunately is disappearing from much of its range as its habitat is developed for housing complexes and parking lots. Excellent and highly recommended, but ONLY if you can buy a captive-bred specimen. The tropical wood turtles, *Rhinoclemmys*, are about eight species of semi-aquatic to purely terrestrial species found from Mexico to central South America. Some are much like the true Wood Turtle in shape and even color, but most have bright head patterns of red and yellow lines and spots. They are intelligent, long-lived if kept warm enough and given bathing facilities, and will take a broad variety of plant and animal foods. Adult *Rhinoclemmys pulcherrima* from Mexico and Central America are excellent pets and very hardy if allowed to bask to their heart's content and given a varied diet with vitamin and calcium supplements. Captive-bred specimens should be purchased if available.

The Laws
Depending on where you are, you probably will need some type of permit to keep a turtle. This may be available through the pet shop or dealer where you purchased the turtle, or you may have to apply through your local department of fish and game or equivalent. Usually permits are inexpensive, but some come with the requirement that you show you know how to maintain a pet.

Because of loss of habitat to development and pollution of water bodies in many countries, it is not recommended that you try to collect your own specimen. Collecting requires a detailed knowledge of local laws and a familiarity with how to identify all the local species so you will not accidentally take protected species. Whenever possible, purchase captive-bred turtles, which put less strain on the natural populations and often do better in captivity and are healthier than wild-caught specimens.

Bibliography

ENCYCLOPEDIA OF TURTLES
By Dr. Peter C. H. Pritchard
ISBN 0-87666-918-6
TFH H-1011
This book is of value to pet keepers, scientific turtle experts, and everyone in between, being particularly mindful of the intelligent general naturalist and the academic zoologist who has use for an overview of the turtles within the covers of a single volume.
Hardcover, 5 1/2 x 8 1/2", 896 pages.
358 color photos, 304 black & white photos, 70 line drawings.

TURTLES FOR HOME AND GARDEN
By Willy Jocher
ISBN 0-87666-777-9
TFH PS-307
This book helps you decide which type of habitat will be easiest to maintain in your locality for keeping shelled reptiles. Extensive instructions given on building outdoor quarters.
Hardcover, 5 1/2 x 8", 128 pages.
32 color photos, 57 black & white photos, 8 line illustrations.

TURTLES AND TERRAPINS:
A Complete Introduction
By Jo Cobb
Hardcvr **CO-026** ISBN 0-86622-275
Softcvr **CO-026S** ISBN 0-86622-280
A completely illustrated, completely practical guide to keeping shelled reptiles of all types successfully, from housing and feeding to helath care and breeding. Dozens of common species are discussed.
5 1/2 x 8 1/2", 128 pages.
Contains 91 full-color photos and 14 full-color illustrations.